MW00621006

Scripture
Memory

———

A BIBLE STUDY COMPANION FROM
THE DAILY GRACE CO.

STEFANIE BOYLES

Contents

Scripture memorization is a spiritual discipline

What is Scripture Memorization?

Scripture memorization is a spiritual discipline—disciplines that traditionally include Bible intake, prayer, fasting, worship, service, fellowship, solitude, and celebration. The powerful discipline of memorizing Scripture falls under Bible intake, as do Scripture meditation and hearing, reading, and studying God's Word. The common goal of these spiritual disciplines is spiritual growth—growing in intimacy with God and being transformed into His likeness. They are a means of grace leading to incredible joy and delight for those who are in Christ.

Specifically, the discipline of Scripture memorization is a spiritual and mental exercise of committing God's Word to memory. While there are various methods we can use in this process, a few unavoidable, common elements are intentional effort, hard work, and repetition. Memorizing Scripture is continually remembering and hiding the Word of God in our hearts so that we can meditate on it day and night. By doing so, we will undoubtedly grow in personal holiness and bear fruit in every season as we allow His living words to work in our hearts and souls. It is a discipline allowing for a deep, transforming connection between the Word of God and the heart and mind of man.

SCRIPTURE MEMORIZATION IS A WORTHY ENDEAVOR FOR EVERY FOLLOWER OF JESUS.

God, in His infinite wisdom, created humans with brains capable of making complex synaptic connections between nerve cells. These connections, formed through frequent and repeated exposure to particular information, reactivate when stored information is called to mind and make memorization possible. The ability to memorize information is a gift, and each of us has the freedom to decide how to exercise this particular gift.

Most of us regularly utilize this God-given capacity as we commit the things we deem as important to our memory banks each day. We memorize our social security numbers, birthdays of friends and family, anniversaries, emergency contact information, dates and times of crucial appointments, lyrics to our favorite songs, and the list goes on. The question is not so much whether we have good memories or enough time and energy—the question is what information is important enough to us that we put in the work needed to establish those connections in our brains?

When it comes to Scripture memorization, we must ask ourselves if we truly value God's Word as important. Do we see the glory of Christ in the Word of God? Do we believe that the Spirit will illuminate the Word and conform us to the image of Christ through it (John 17:17)? Do we believe that God's Word is nourishment to our souls and all we need for life and godliness (2 Peter 1:3)? If we do not value Scripture, we will lack the discipline to continually subject ourselves to its words by committing them to memory. In turn, we miss out on enjoying the fruit produced from the deep connection between God's Word and our hearts and minds.

WHAT VALUE DO YOU PLACE ON GOD'S WORD?

HOW DOES YOUR LIFE TESTIFY TO THE VALUE YOU
PUT ON SCRIPTURE?

Why Scripture Memory is a Worthy Endeavor

THE BIBLE IS THE WORD OF GOD

The Bible is not an ordinary book, nor is it an inspiring work of art that withstands the test of time like Homer's *Iliad* or Plato's *The Republic*. While the accuracy of the Bible has been affirmed by more ancient manuscripts than any other writing, the Bible is different because it is not a product of men (1 Thessalonians 2:13)—rather, every word inside is inspired by God (2 Timothy 3:16). While God employed over forty men to physically write down the words of Scripture, He provided the content.

The Bible is "living and effective" even today (Hebrews 4:12). Not only does God's Word have the power to search our hearts and expose our deepest thoughts, intentions, desires, and sins, but it is the primary means by which God reveals Himself — we find wisdom in heeding His words. We do not need to look for special revelation because the Bible is all we need for life and godliness (2 Peter 1:3), its wisdom and truth offering sufficient principles to guide us through all of life's circumstances.

Scripture memorization is its own separate discipline for good reason. As we exercise our minds with the goal of retention, we will inevitably find that we go more deeply into the text. And as we repetitively engage with the verses, our understanding of the passage will increase. We will better grasp the author's original intent and be more equipped to accurately apply its principles to our everyday lives. Furthermore, we will find memorization to be a tool that allows us to meditate on Scripture day and night as it works its way from our heads to our hearts.

(2)

OUR SANCTIFICATION

Many verses throughout the Bible highlight the discipline of Scripture memorization. We find that memorizing Scripture is actively treasuring God's commands (Proverbs 7:1), storing up His words in our hearts (Psalm 119:11), allowing His words to remain in us (John 15:7), and having His words in our hearts so that we can teach them to our children (Deuteronomy 6:4-9). While memorizing Scripture may not be explicitly commanded in the Bible, it is abundantly evident that it has played a noteworthy role in the spiritual life of God's people throughout the ages.

When we treasure His Word and store it up in our hearts, we are essentially working for our good. Deuteronomy 10:13 says, "Keep the Lord's commands and statutes I am giving you today, for your own good." Allowing the Word of God to inform and shape our thoughts, feelings, and actions is how we live as God intended, which is better than anything our sin-sick world has to offer. However, for His Word to direct our lives, we must allow it to take hold of us and shape us. We need His Words to wholly sink in, transforming our hopes and desires. But this does not happen from a casual readthrough of Scripture.

As we memorize Scripture, we give way to the discipline of Scripture meditation that allows God's Words to move from our heads to our hearts. The Holy Spirit sanctifies us through His Word by illuminating it in such a way that we can see absolute truth, and He often uses those verses that are readily available in the recesses of our minds as we go about our days. Through them, He reminds us of the promises of God and helps us apply those biblical truths and principles. Memorizing Scripture is profitable for our edification and sanctification.

LIVING IN THE "ALREADY, BUT NOT YET"

This world is broken. Sin has marred God's creation and distorted His good design for mankind. Each of us is well acquainted with the effects of the fall. We have faced trials, suffering, pain, death, disease, and all forms of dissonance. However, God has not left us alone. He has given us His indwelling Spirit and the armor of God (Ephesians 6:10-18). Our weapon of offense in this armor is the sword of the Spirit, which is the Word of God. To reap the benefits of this weapon, we need to wield it. We need to always have it with us, and we need the ability to use it. His Word and an understanding of its contents should be readily available in our minds so that we can effectively use it in battle. In this way, we will be equipped at any moment to fight spiritual warfare and victoriously face the reality of our fallen world.

Memorizing Scripture strengthens us inwardly. When our minds are filled with His Word, we have a line of defense from sinning against Him (Psalm 119:11). When we grow weary, our hearts can be strengthened and comforted by His promises. No matter what circumstances we face, the Spirit can call His Word to our minds, as needed, whether to bring about conviction or encouragement. We may also find that our prayer lives will be deepened as our minds are saturated by His Word. Rather than using the same words and phrases to bring about our petitions before the Lord, we can pray His words back to Him, using the language of Scripture in both our lament and our praise.

The Bible is "living and effective" even today.

Common Objections to Memorizing Scripture

Scripture memorization is a spiritual discipline for every believer—not just for the seminary student, Bible teacher, missionary, or pastor. However, it requires work. Committing anything to memory is a mental exercise for anyone up for the task. While some people may have a photographic memory, the vast majority do not, and this discipline takes time and patience. There are helpful strategies one can utilize, but the bottom line is, memorizing requires repetition, perseverance, and will.

Because memorization is not an easy task, it helps to confront some of the most common excuses people use to forfeit the endeavor. It is better to rehearse these objections from the very beginning so we quickly recognize them when they cross our minds when the going gets tough.

COMMON EXCUSES

1. "I HAVE A BAD MEMORY."

2. "I'M NOT IN THE RIGHT SEASON OF LIFE."

3. "I HAVE NO TIME."

4. "I ALWAYS HAVE MY PHONE ON ME, SO THE BIBLE IS ALWAYS ACCESSIBLE."

5. "MEMORIZATION IS A LOST ART."

6. "I'M NOT IN VOCATIONAL MINISTRY."

7. "ISN'T READING AND STUDYING
   SCRIPTURE ENOUGH?"

8. "I DON'T KNOW WHAT TO MEMORIZE."

9. "I CAN'T EVEN MEMORIZE ONE VERSE —
   HOW AM I SUPPOSED TO MEMORIZE A
   WHOLE PASSAGE, CHAPTER, OR BOOK?"

10. "I HAVE NO DESIRE TO MEMORIZE."

Although we are wholly redeemed in Christ, we still wrestle with our sinful flesh. On this side of eternity, the Christian life is a continual battle of the heart's affections. However, through the hard work of everyday faithfulness comes the soul-satisfying joy of a fruitful life in Him!

WHAT EXCUSE HAVE YOU FOUND YOURSELF USING
TO JUSTIFY NOT MEMORIZING SCRIPTURE?

①

LACK OF TIME

Having a deep-seated desire to know and love God through Scripture memorization will carry us further than a sharp memory. A good memory helps store up information, but a desire to be conformed to the image of Christ transforms memorization into spiritual formation. Love for God is what will help us persevere and keep our hands on the plow. The Lord preserves His people and welcomes us to come to Him in our need. So when we feel discouraged by our mental capabilities to memorize Scripture, we can pray and ask God to increase our capacity to do so.

Every season of life is a season for God's Word. Matthew 4:4 tells us, "Man must not live on bread alone but on every word that comes from the mouth of God." His Word is our daily bread. Just as food sustains our physical bodies, His Word is sustenance for our souls. This is why we cannot neglect spiritual disciplines in busier seasons of life. Maybe we are in the throes of newborn days or the middle of a college semester. Maybe we are learning a new job, preparing to move across the state or country, or caring for a sick loved one. We feel like our capacity to focus and memorize is even further diminished because our minds seem to be running in a hundred different directions. However, these busy seasons are precisely the seasons we need God's Word stored in our hearts. When our brains are overloaded or foggy, what a gift to have familiar verses and passages stored in our hearts that can minister to us as they are brought to mind.

Even though it may be more laborious or slow to commit His Word to memory, let us press on in this endeavor, knowing it is for our good. Scripture memorization is not a competition. Whether we memorize one verse a day, one verse a week, or one verse a month, it is well worth our time.

EVEN IF WE DO NOT THINK WE WILL PERSONALLY USE THESE COMMON EXCUSES, IT IS WISE TO HAVE TRUTHS READY IN CASE THEY COME UP. WRITE A ONE-SENTENCE TRUTH STATEMENT TO COMBAT EACH OF THESE EXCUSES.

1. "I HAVE A BAD MEMORY."

2. "I'M NOT IN THE RIGHT SEASON OF LIFE."

3. "I HAVE NO TIME."

Memorization may feel like a lost art today. Many of us always have our phones within arm's reach — search engines and endless streams of information are at our fingertips. This also means the Bible is readily accessible to us. If not already downloaded on our phones, many of us have multiple copies of God's Word on our bookshelves. While it is a profound blessing to have the whole counsel of God so readily accessible, a potential danger is the undervaluing of memorization and study.

Just because something is accessible does not mean it is utilized. Information is only helpful when it is retrieved, understood, and appropriately applied. The same is true for God's Word. If we read Scripture but ignore the study, meditation, and memorization associated with the discipline of Bible intake, we miss out on experiencing the fullness of its intended purpose in our lives. Committing Scripture to memory not only allows us to have continual access to it, but when it is stored in our hearts and minds, the Spirit can use it to sanctify us (John 17:17) — to admonish us, encourage us, comfort us, convict us, lead us, and shape and inform our consciences..

Scripture memorization can also increase our confidence and effectiveness in evangelism and discipleship, neither of which are tasks relegated only to pastors; every disciple of Jesus is called to make disciples (Matthew 28:16-20). Professing believers should be able and ready to give a defense for the hope they have in Christ (1 Peter 3:15). This means that each of us needs to have some level of gospel fluency. We need the ability to communicate the truths found in Scripture without relying on our phones.

Reading and studying Scripture are spiritual disciplines necessary for every believer, and they are the means for us to know God. He uses the Word to renew our minds (Romans 12:2). Scripture memorization is the discipline that deepens the connection between the Word and the heart and mind of man. It bridges the gap between study and meditation, which leads to a deeper understanding of God's Word and appropriate application to life. Every spiritual discipline is worth our time and effort!

EVEN IF WE DO NOT THINK WE WILL PERSONALLY USE THESE COMMON EXCUSES, IT IS WISE TO HAVE TRUTHS READY IN CASE THEY COME UP. WRITE A ONE-SENTENCE TRUTH STATEMENT TO COMBAT EACH OF THESE EXCUSES.

4. "I ALWAYS HAVE MY PHONE ON ME, SO THE BIBLE IS ALWAYS ACCESSIBLE."

5. "MEMORIZATION IS A LOST ART."

6. "I'M NOT IN VOCATIONAL MINISTRY."

7. "ISN'T READING AND STUDYING SCRIPTURE ENOUGH?"

A major barrier to pursuing anything is knowing where to start. When it comes to beginning the journey of memorizing Scripture, many people feel paralyzed. After all, there are over 31,000 verses in the Bible. All of the different genres, cultures, and time periods can seem intimidating. But the Lord is gracious, and we can trust that His Word will accomplish the work that He purposes in our lives (Isaiah 55:11). This does not mean that we cannot systematically approach Scripture memory. There are various ways to approach Scripture memorization, many of which will be shared in this resource.

No matter what methodology we use, we want to remember a few things. First, we should always be aware of context—careful never to pull verses out of the intended context and misapply promises or principles. This is one reason it is helpful to memorize larger passages or whole chapters. Second, a methodology is powerless to change our hearts and renew our minds. We should approach this spiritual discipline with the desire to know more of who God is, fully depending on the Spirit to conform us to the image of Christ through His Word.

Not knowing where to begin is different than lacking the desire to memorize Scripture. Jesus makes it clear in John 15 that abiding in Him involves His words abiding in us. Evidence of our union with Him is obedience to His Word (John 15:10). If we want to obey His Word, we must know and treasure His Word. Just like real-life relationships in which our love for the people in our lives is intimately tethered to our knowledge of them, so it is for our relationship with God! Our love for Him increases as our knowledge of Him grows.

EVEN IF WE DO NOT THINK WE WILL PERSONALLY USE
THESE COMMON EXCUSES, IT IS WISE TO HAVE TRUTHS
READY IN CASE THEY COME UP. WRITE A ONE-SENTENCE
TRUTH STATEMENT TO COMBAT EACH OF THESE EXCUSES.

8. "I DON'T KNOW WHAT TO MEMORIZE."

_____

_____

_____

_____

9. "I CAN'T EVEN MEMORIZE ONE VERSE — HOW AM
    I SUPPOSED TO MEMORIZE A WHOLE PASSAGE,
    CHAPTER, OR BOOK?"

_____

_____

_____

_____

10. "I HAVE NO DESIRE TO MEMORIZE."

_____

_____

_____

_____

THE LORD IS GRACIOUS, AND WE CAN TRUST
THAT HIS WORD WILL ACCOMPLISH THE WORK
THAT HE PURPOSES IN OUR LIVES.

5 Baldness has come upon Gaza;
   Ashkelon has perished.
O remnant of their valley,
   how long will you gash yourselves?
6 Ah, sword of the LORD!
   How long till you are quiet?
Put yourself into your scabbard;
   rest and be still!
7 How can it¹ be quiet
   when the LORD has given it a charge?
Against Ashkelon and against the sea-
      shore
   he has appointed it."

Judgment on Moab

48 Concerning Moab.
Thus says the LORD of hosts, the God
of Israel:

   "Woe to Nebo, for it is laid waste!
      Kiriathaim is put to shame, it is
         taken;
   the fortress is put to shame and broken
         down;
2   the renown of Moab is no more.
   In Heshbon they planned disaster against
         her:
      'Come, let us cut her off from being a
         nation!'
   You also, O Madmen, shall be brought to
         silence;
      the sword shall pursue you.
3 "A voice! A cry from Horonaim!
      'Desolation and great destruction!
4 Moab is destroyed;
      ᵗˢ have made a cry.

   the valley shall perish,
      and the plain shall be destroyed,
   as the LORD has spoken.
9 "Give wings to Moab,
      for she would fly away,
   her cities shall become a desolation,
      with no inhabitant in them.

10 "Cursed is he who does the work of the
   LORD with slackness, and cursed is he who
   keeps back his sword from bloodshed.

11 "Moab has been at ease from his youth
      and has settled on his dregs,
   he has not been emptied from vessel to ves-
         sel,
      nor has he gone into exile;
   so his taste remains in him,
      and his scent is not changed.

12 "Therefore, behold, the days are coming,
   declares the LORD, when I shall send to him
   pourers who will pour him, and empty his ves-
   sels and break his² jars in pieces. ¹³Then Moab
   shall be ashamed of Chemosh, as the house of
   Israel was ashamed of Bethel, their confidence.

14 "How do you say, 'We are heroes
      and mighty men of war'?
15 The destroyer of Moab and his cities has
         come up,
   and the choicest of his young men have
      gone down to slaughter,
   declares the King, whose name is the
      LORD of hosts.
16 The calamity of Moab is near at hand,
      and his affliction hastens swiftly.
17 Grieve for him, all you who are around
         him,
      and all who know his name;
   say, 'How the mighty scepter is broken,
      ᵗⁱᵒᵘˢ staff!'

JEREMIAH 49:1

If we want to obey His Word, we must know and treasure His Word.

⁷"For every head is shaved and every beard
off. On all the hands are gashes, and around
the waist is sackcloth. ³⁸ On all the housetops of
Moab and in the squares there is nothing but
lamentation, for I have broken Moab like a vessel
for which no one cares, declares the LORD. ³⁹ How
it is broken! How they wail! How Moab has
turned his back in shame! So Moab has become a
derision and a horror to all that are around him."

⁴⁰ For thus says the LORD:
"Behold, one shall fly swiftly like an eagle
   and spread his wings against Moab;
⁴¹ the cities shall be taken
   and the strongholds seized.
The heart of the warriors of Moab shall be
   in that day
like the heart of a woman in her birth
   pains;
⁴² Moab shall be destroyed and be no longer
   a people,
because he magnified himself against
   the LORD.
⁴³ Terror, pit, and snare
   are before you, O inhabitant of Moab!
      declares the LORD.
⁴⁴ He who flees from the terror
   shall fall into the pit,
and he who climbs out of the pit
   shall be caught in the snare.
For I will bring these things upon Moab,
   the year of their punishment,
      declares the LORD.

⁴⁵ "In the shadow of Heshbon
   fugitives stop without strength,
for fire came out from Heshbon,
   flame from the house of Sihon;
it has destroyed the forehead of Moab,
   the crown of the sons of tumult.
⁴⁶ Woe to you, O Moab!
   The people of Chemosh are undone,
for your sons have been taken captive,
   and your daughters into captivity.
⁴⁷ Yet I will restore the fortunes of Moab
   in the latter days, declares the LORD."
Thus far is the judgment on Moab.

What Verses or Passages Should We Memorize?

Choosing which verses or passages to memorize can sometimes stand as a challenge—how do we decide on one verse if every verse is important? We can consider a number of ideas. When memorizing individual verses, it is helpful to pull them from books of the Bible we are currently reading or have studied in the past. Overlapping our reading and studying material with our memorization will enrich each of the individual spiritual disciplines.

We can also consider choosing verses topically. Examples of topics include verses for your struggles, verses of comfort in times of suffering, or verses that remind you of God's character and promises. Another approach is to memorize prayers found throughout Scripture that we too can lift up to the Lord or use as a model for our own prayers. Maybe there is simply a verse or passage the Spirit has impressed upon us that we want to be able to easily call to mind.

It is important to remember, however, that while no one way is necessarily better than the other, regardless of which approach we use for Scripture memorization, we must safeguard against pulling biblical texts out of context. This means that we need to have a general understanding of the surrounding passage of any verse we memorize and subsequently use for encouragement. To the best of our abilities, we want to be faithful to the text, accurately applying it to our lives. No matter what Scripture we memorize or the approach we use to do so, we can be confident knowing that all "Scripture is inspired by God and profitable…" (2 Timothy 3:16), and as the Word of God, it will accomplish what the Lord intends (Isaiah 55:11).

WE HAVE THE FREEDOM TO MEMORIZE INDIVIDUAL VERSES. WHAT ARE SOME THINGS YOU CAN DO TO MAKE SURE YOU ARE KEEPING THEM IN THE APPROPRIATE CONTEXT?

MEMORIZING INDIVIDUAL VERSES

Many promises of God throughout the Bible can deeply encourage us. We should not let the fear of pulling these verses out of context discourage us from hiding His Word in our hearts. There is power in awareness and wisdom in putting up safeguards. If you want to explore and memorize verses that you are not currently reading or studying, the following are a few categories to consider.

VERSES SHOWCASING THE CHARACTER OF GOD

☐ *Revelation 1:8*   ☐ *2 Timothy 2:13*
☐ *Psalm 34:8*   ☐ *Hebrews 13:8*
☐ *Colossians 1:17*

VERSES ENCAPSULATING GOSPEL TRUTHS

☐ *Romans 5:8*   ☐ *Romans 6:23*
☐ *Romans 8:1*   ☐ *2 Corinthians 5:21*
☐ *1 John 4:10*

VERSES EXPOUNDING ON THE CHRISTIAN LIFE

☐ *1 John 3:18*   ☐ *1 Peter 2:11*
☐ *Galatians 6:9-10* ☐ *Philippians 2:3-4*
☐ *Ephesians 5:2*

The Daily Grace Company has many Scripture card sets that speak to different life circumstances.

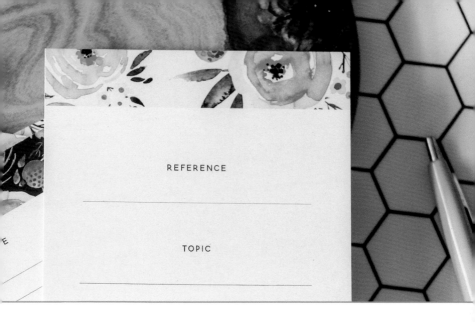

REFERENCE

_____

TOPIC

_____

VERSES FOR DIFFERENT SEASONS

PREGNANCY
- ☐ *Colossians 1:16-17*
- ☐ *Psalm 139:13-14*
- ☐ *2 Corinthians 12:9*

GRIEF
- ☐ *Psalm 34:18*
- ☐ *Psalm 73:26*
- ☐ *Revelation 21:4*

MARRIAGE
- ☐ *Matthew 19:6*
- ☐ *1 Thessalonians 5:23-24*
- ☐ *1 Corinthians 13:4-7*

ANXIETY
- ☐ *Psalm 56:8-9*
- ☐ *Psalm 42:5*
- ☐ *Philippians 4:6-7*

CONSIDER YOUR CURRENT LIFE SEASON AND CIRCUMSTANCES. TAKE SOME TIME TO WRITE OUT SPECIFIC VERSE REFERENCES THAT YOU WOULD LIKE TO COMMIT TO MEMORY.

WHAT ARE SOME VERSES YOU WOULD LIKE TO MEMORIZE THAT PRESENT THE GOSPEL?

MEMORIZING LARGER PASSAGES

Scripture memorization is hard as it requires intentional effort, consistency, and mental energy. This can make the idea of memorizing individual verses, let alone larger passages, seem daunting. Yet, some people regularly memorize entire books of the Bible—ordinary people who have, over time, developed the ability to recite extended passages. Memorizing Scripture, especially at length, is not easy; however, like any discipline, the more we exercise these particular muscles, the stronger they become.

There are tremendous benefits of memorizing entire chapters and books of the Bible. This approach is the safest way to protect against pulling verses out of context as it helps keep us from overlooking connecting verses and better grasp the author's intended flow of thought. Slowly, as verses build upon each other in our memory, we can see how verses purposefully fit into paragraphs, paragraphs into chapters, and chapters into books. In the end, we will have a greater understanding of how these individual books fit into the greater story of redemption.

Endeavoring to memorize larger passages requires diligence, but it helps us rightly handle God's Word (2 Timothy 2:15). We are less likely to isolate certain verses to serve our own purposes and instead, value the intent of the book's divine author. We are able to apply biblical principles appropriately in our lives and teach others to do likewise. What a beautiful way to edify the body of Christ at large!

BE DILIGENT TO PRESENT YOURSELF TO GOD AS ONE
APPROVED, A WORKER WHO DOESN'T NEED TO BE
ASHAMED, CORRECTLY TEACHING THE WORD OF TRUTH.

2 TIMOTHY 2:15

HAVE YOU EVER CONSIDERED MEMORIZING A LARGER PASSAGE OF SCRIPTURE — AN ENTIRE CHAPTER OR AN ENTIRE BOOK OF THE BIBLE? IF SO, HAVE YOU DONE IT? SHARE YOUR EXPERIENCE! IF NOT, WHAT HAS PREVENTED YOU FROM TRYING IT OUT?

MEMORIZING VERSE REFERENCES

The original authors of each book of the Bible did not include chapter and verse numbers. In fact, verse notations were not added until the 13th century to ease the burden of referencing specific portions of the Bible in commentaries. If opting to include the references in our memorization for each individual verse, it is incredibly helpful to memorize the reference first and then the verse. This is particularly helpful if memorizing an assortment of verses from different books of the Bible.

EXAMPLE: EPHESIANS 1:1-3

Recite the passage below omitting the verse numbers.

> *Ephesians 1*
> *Paul, an apostle of Christ Jesus by God's will: To the faithful saints in Christ Jesus at Ephesus. Grace to you and peace from God our Father and the Lord Jesus Christ. Blessed is the God and Father of our Lord Jesus Christ, who has blessed us with every spiritual blessing in the heavens in Christ.*

Now, recite the passage below including the verse numbers.

> *Ephesians 1:1*
> *Paul, an apostle of Christ Jesus by God's will: To the faithful saints in Christ Jesus at Ephesus.*
>
> *Ephesians 1:2*
> *Grace to you and peace from God our Father and the Lord Jesus Christ.*
>
> *Ephesians 1:3*
> *Blessed is the God and Father of our Lord Jesus Christ, who has blessed us with every spiritual blessing in the heavens in Christ.*

For the Word to direct our lives, we must allow it to take hold of us and shape us.

Choosing a Bible Translation

When committing Scripture to memory, it is helpful to stick to one translation. If you are new to memorizing Scripture, take some time to think about which translation you want to use. Below is a chart to help you decide, but you will probably want to choose the translation you typically read and study. We recommend avoiding paraphrases and instead choosing a translation that falls somewhere between word-for-word and thought-for-thought. The Daily Grace Co. primarily uses ESV and CSB.

TRANSLATION COMPARISON

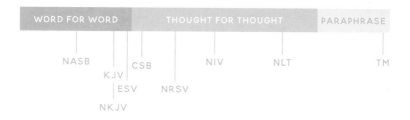

NASB *North American Standard Bible*
KJV *King James Version*
NKJV *New King James Version*
ESV *English Standard Version*
CSB *Christian Standard Bible*

NRSV *New Revised Standard Version*
NIV *New International Version*
NLT *New Living Translation*
TM *The Message*

Where Do We Start?

Scripture memorization is both a mental and spiritual exercise. We never want to pursue knowledge of God for knowledge's sake. First Corinthians 8:1 says, "knowledge puffs up, but love builds up." Although knowledge of God's Word is necessary for growing in spiritual maturity, it should never be isolated from the love of God and the magnification of His glory. So as we pursue personal holiness through the practice of the spiritual disciplines, we cannot forget to evaluate our hearts. Our greatest desire should be more of Christ.

As we evaluate our hearts, we also want to engage in any spiritual discipline with prayer. We begin with prayer, are sustained by prayer, and respond in prayer. Before we even select which verse or passage to store in our minds, we can pray, inviting the Lord into the process as we seek His wisdom and guidance.

OUR GREATEST DESIRE SHOULD
BE MORE OF CHRIST.

WRITE OUT A PRAYER, INVITING GOD INTO THIS PROCESS AND ASKING HIM TO HELP YOU IDENTIFY WHICH VERSES OR PASSAGES WOULD BE MOST PERSONALLY EDIFYING FOR YOU RIGHT NOW.

As we consider the verse or passages we would like to commit to memory, we should remember that like with anything else in life—even the very best intentions often fall to the wayside without a plan, so come up with a plan before you begin! Challenge yourself while also being realistic so as not to get discouraged.

START WITH A PLAN

PICK A LIST OF VERSES, OR SELECT A
CHAPTER OR BOOK OF THE BIBLE.

CONSIDER YOUR MENTAL CAPACITIES,
LIFE SEASON, AND AVAILABILITY AS YOU
DECIDE ON REALISTIC, MEASURABLE
GOALS (E.G., ONE VERSE A DAY,
ONE VERSE A WEEK, ETC.).

WRITE OUT YOUR GOAL.

WRITE OUT THE TARGET DATE THAT
YOU WANT TO ACCOMPLISH YOUR OVERALL
GOAL BY (INCLUDING SOME WIGGLE ROOM).

Perhaps you decide to memorize the book of Ephesians. Ephesians has six chapters with a total of 155 verses. Because you are in a busy season of life and feel like your mental capacity is low, your goal is to memorize one verse a week. This means that it will take you 155 weeks to accomplish your goal—two years and nine months. Allowing wiggle room, you set your target date for three years from your start date. Indeed, this is a long-term investment, but what great benefit and joy are found in storing away His Word as treasure in your heart. Like the Christian life, we should have a long-term perspective and be committed to everyday faithfulness.

SAMPLE PLAN

SELECTION: EPHESIANS

6 CHAPTERS = 155 VERSES

GOAL: 1 VERSE A WEEK

{155 WEEKS}

TARGET DATE: 3 YEARS FROM TODAY

Your Plan

WHETHER YOU HAVE DECIDED TO MEMORIZE A SHORT
PASSAGE OR AN ENTIRE BOOK OF THE BIBLE, IT IS TIME
TO WRITE OUT THE SPECIFICS OF YOUR PLAN!

I COMMIT TO MEMORIZING:

_____

CONSIDERING MY LIFE SEASON, THE REALISTIC AND

MEASURABLE GOAL I AM SETTING FOR MYSELF IS TO

MEMORIZE _____ VERSE(S) EVERY WEEK.

MY TARGET END GOAL DATE (INCLUDING

WIGGLE ROOM) IS _____.

Right Perspective & Learning Style

The Christian life requires a long-term perspective and commitment to everyday faithfulness—it is not a sprint but more like an ultra-marathon. We can view memorizing Scripture as one way of consistently fueling ourselves for sustenance in this race. Some days will feel easier, like trotting downhill, and other days will be harder. However, every step forward counts, and this is also true of ordinary, everyday faithfulness. As believers, we must fix our eyes on the prize that is eternity with Christ.

With this right perspective, no matter what approach to Scripture memory we use, repetition is key. God created our brains to establish the neural pathways necessary to recall information, and we need this particular form of mental exercise as our minds will be tempted to be disinterested and lazy. Be committed to strengthening these particular muscles every single day!

Identifying how we learn best is helpful too. Because all of us are created differently, we process information best when it is presented in a learning style specific to each of us. The broad categories for learning style include visual, auditory/musical, kinesthetic/physical, and verbal. Each of these categories breaks down further to encompass different methods of application, depending on the learner.

WE MUST FIX OUR EYES ON THE PRIZE THAT IS ETERNITY WITH CHRIST.

VISUAL

Write the verses on index cards, and place them where you will see them frequently.

Write the verses or first letter of each word of the verses on your hand or wrist.

Carry a printed copy of the verses in your purse to review whenever possible.

KINESTHETIC / PHYSICAL

Write out the verses over and over again.

Create motions to accompany main words in the verses.

Chant the verses with claps or stomps.

Write each word of the verses on separate slips of paper, mix them up, then place them back in order.

AUDITORY / MUSICAL

Listen to the verses on repeat through an audio Bible app.

Record yourself reading the verses on a voice memo, and listen to it over and over again.

Put the verse to music, and sing it.

VERBAL

Repeat the verses over and over again out loud.

Read the verses repetitively, and cover words as you progress.

Say the verses out loud to a friend or spouse.

Teach the verse to someone else.

HOW BEST DO YOU LEARN?

HOW DO YOU PREFER INFORMATION TO BE
PRESENTED TO YOU?

KNOWING THIS, WHAT METHODS DO YOU THINK WOULD
BE MOST HELPFUL AS YOU MEMORIZE SCRIPTURE?

*Some of us may find that using multiple strategies will help cement the verses
in our memory, or we may need to use trial and error to find the method that
works best. Once identifying our strongest learning style and finding a strategy
within that category, we can try combining it with one or two other strategies
to employ a multi-sensory approach. While some of us prefer one learning
style over another, we would all benefit from engaging each of our different
senses to store large amounts of information. We can get creative here!*

Other Ideas

MEMORIZING IS BETTER TOGETHER.

Memorize versees with friends or family. Accountability is powerful! Commit to either emailing each other weekly to check in or sending a voice memo through a text message or an audio or video app.

FIT IT IN YOUR MORNING ROUTINE.

Print out the verses on a piece of paper, and slip it into a zip lock bag to post in the shower. Pro tip: put the zip-up seal on the bottom so water will not seep in!

USE SOME SCREEN TIME.

Set verses as your phone's lock screen so you see them every time you pick up your phone.

USE AN APP.

Download a Scripture memory app on your phone if possible. A number of these are available and easy to use.

DIVE DEEP INTO THE TEXT.

Use a blank notebook to write out the verses and what they mean, or find guidance from resources like the Dwell Scripture Memory Journal from The Daily Grace Co. that walk you through memorizing longer passages while offering word studies to deepen your understanding of the text you are memorizing. It is easier to memorize something when you understand the teaching and principles behind it.

CHOOSE AN ANCHOR ACTIVITY.

Couple Scripture memory (and other spiritual disciplines!) with already existing anchors in your day. This could be eating breakfast, going on a walk or using the elliptical, waiting in a car line, putting on make-up or taking a shower, washing the dishes, etc. Choose an anchor, and commit to reviewing or learning new memory verses during that time.

WHAT SPECIFIC STRATEGIES STICK OUT TO YOU?

IS THERE AN ANCHOR IN YOUR DAY YOU CAN COUPLE WITH
THE DISCIPLINE OF SCRIPTURE MEMORIZATION?

Review & Retention

In order to retain information over the long haul, we need to store information in our long-term memory banks. Continual repetition is the best way to create stronger neural connections, especially when we interact with the information through different sensory modalities (visual, auditory, kinesthetic, and verbal). Furthermore, frequently recalling the information and applying it to our lives is also helpful. As students of the Word, this can happen naturally as we engage with the Word every day. However, it is helpful to have some sort of review system to retain what we commit to memory.

REVIEW MODEL FOR INDIVIDUAL VERSES
(ONE VERSE A WEEK)

Memorize the verse according to the plan you have set for the week.

↓

Once you have memorized the verse, commit to reviewing it every day for fifty days.

↓

Add a new verse each week, repeating this process for each of them.

↓

After the fifty days of review for each verse, commit to reviewing them once a week for fifty weeks.
Then, move your review to every one to two months.

Memorize the first verse of the passage the first week.

↓

The next week, add the second verse, still reciting the first verse daily as well. Repeat this process, adding the next new verse each week.

↓

Continue this process until every verse of the passage is committed to memory. On the very last day, you should be reciting the entire passage or book.

↓

Recite the entire book every day for at least a month (some recommend reciting it daily for several months!).

While there is surely merit in retaining verses and passages we memorize, some choose to memorize an entire book of the Bible and move on to another with no intention of remembering the previous passage word for word. Yet, this approach is still tremendously beneficial as the deeper understanding of the previous book will always remain. How valuable is the spiritual formation that takes place through the process of hiding God's Word in our hearts!

IN YOUR OWN WORDS, WHAT IS THE VALUE OF
MEMORIZING SCRIPTURE?

Sing the verses, pray the verses, teach the verses.

Words of Encouragement

As we practice spiritual disciplines like Scripture memorization, we should do so with prayer, inviting the Lord into the process, asking daily for His help—that He will sustain us in our pursuit of knowing Him through His Word. We pray as the psalmist cries out in Psalm 119:18, "Open my eyes so that I may contemplate wondrous things from your instruction." We come to Him humbly, asking Him to keep us in a posture of humility throughout the journey.

Our spiritual appetite for God may sometimes be faint, but we trust that the best thing to do is continue feasting on His Word as we commit it to memory. Say the verses out loud! Gaining a better understanding of the context and meaning, say the verses with heart! Sing the verses, pray the verses, teach the verses to friends and family!

OPEN MY EYES SO THAT I MAY COMTEMPLATE
WONDROUS THINGS FROM YOUR INSTRUCTION.

PSALM 119:18

WRITE A NOTE TO YOURSELF EXPLAINING WHY YOU
WANT TO MEMORIZE SCRIPTURE. WHY DOES IT MAKE
YOU EXCITED? HOW ARE YOU HOPING TO GROW? THIS
WILL BE A PEP TALK FOR YOURSELF TO COME BACK TO
ON A DISCOURAGING DAY.

In the end, we can trust that *the Lord will grow us and bear fruit in and through us* for His glory.

His Word has the power to *change us and mold us,* and when we faithfully memorize His Word, we will have access to its power at any time.

Memorizing Scripture is for every believer, and it is a worthy endeavor!

Scripture Memory Tracker

PASSAGE: _____

TOPIC: _____

STARTED ON: _____ MEMORIZED ON: _____

PASSAGE: _____

TOPIC: _____

STARTED ON: _____ MEMORIZED ON: _____

PASSAGE: _____

TOPIC: _____

STARTED ON: _____ MEMORIZED ON: _____

PASSAGE: _____

TOPIC: _____

STARTED ON: _____ MEMORIZED ON: _____

PASSAGE: _____

TOPIC: _____

STARTED ON: _____ MEMORIZED ON: _____

PASSAGE: _____

TOPIC: _____

STARTED ON: _____ MEMORIZED ON: _____

PASSAGE:_____

TOPIC:_____

STARTED ON:_____ MEMORIZED ON:_____

PASSAGE:_____

TOPIC:_____

STARTED ON:_____ MEMORIZED ON:_____

PASSAGE:_____

TOPIC:_____

STARTED ON:_____ MEMORIZED ON:_____

PASSAGE:_____

TOPIC:_____

STARTED ON:_____ MEMORIZED ON:_____

PASSAGE:_____

TOPIC:_____

STARTED ON:_____ MEMORIZED ON:_____

PASSAGE:_____

TOPIC:_____

STARTED ON:_____ MEMORIZED ON:_____

PASSAGE: _____

TOPIC: _____

STARTED ON: _____ MEMORIZED ON: _____

PASSAGE: _____

TOPIC: _____

STARTED ON: _____ MEMORIZED ON: _____

PASSAGE: _____

TOPIC: _____

STARTED ON: _____ MEMORIZED ON: _____

PASSAGE: _____

TOPIC: _____

STARTED ON: _____ MEMORIZED ON: _____

PASSAGE: _____

TOPIC: _____

STARTED ON: _____ MEMORIZED ON: _____

PASSAGE: _____

TOPIC: _____

STARTED ON: _____ MEMORIZED ON: _____

PASSAGE: _____

TOPIC: _____

STARTED ON: _____ MEMORIZED ON: _____

PASSAGE:_____

TOPIC:_____

STARTED ON:_____ MEMORIZED ON:_____

PASSAGE:_____

TOPIC:_____

STARTED ON:_____ MEMORIZED ON:_____

PASSAGE:_____

TOPIC:_____

STARTED ON:_____ MEMORIZED ON:_____

PASSAGE:_____

TOPIC:_____

STARTED ON:_____ MEMORIZED ON:_____

PASSAGE:_____

TOPIC:_____

STARTED ON:_____ MEMORIZED ON:_____

PASSAGE:_____

TOPIC:_____

STARTED ON:_____ MEMORIZED ON:_____

PASSAGE:_____

TOPIC:_____

STARTED ON:_____ MEMORIZED ON:_____

PASSAGE:_____

TOPIC:_____

STARTED ON:_____ MEMORIZED ON:_____

PASSAGE:_____

TOPIC:_____

STARTED ON:_____ MEMORIZED ON:_____

PASSAGE:_____

TOPIC:_____

STARTED ON:_____ MEMORIZED ON:_____

PASSAGE:_____

TOPIC:_____

STARTED ON:_____ MEMORIZED ON:_____

PASSAGE:_____

TOPIC:_____

STARTED ON:_____ MEMORIZED ON:_____

PASSAGE:_____

TOPIC:_____

STARTED ON:_____ MEMORIZED ON:_____

PASSAGE:_____

TOPIC:_____

STARTED ON:_____ MEMORIZED ON:_____

PASSAGE: _____

TOPIC: _____

STARTED ON: _____ MEMORIZED ON: _____

PASSAGE: _____

TOPIC: _____

STARTED ON: _____ MEMORIZED ON: _____

PASSAGE: _____

TOPIC: _____

STARTED ON: _____ MEMORIZED ON: _____

PASSAGE: _____

TOPIC: _____

STARTED ON: _____ MEMORIZED ON: _____

PASSAGE: _____

TOPIC: _____

STARTED ON: _____ MEMORIZED ON: _____

PASSAGE: _____

TOPIC: _____

STARTED ON: _____ MEMORIZED ON: _____

PASSAGE: _____

TOPIC: _____

STARTED ON: _____ MEMORIZED ON: _____

Thank you for choosing this resource from The Daily Grace Co.

CONNECT WITH US

@thedailygraceco
@kristinschmucker

CONTACT US

info@thedailygraceco.com

SHARE

#thedailygraceco
#lampandlight

VISIT US ONLINE

www.thedailygraceco.com

MORE DAILY GRACE

The Daily Grace app
Daily Grace podcast